Albert Pujols

By Jeff Savage

AMAZING ATHLETES

Lerner Publications Company • Minneapolis

Lerner Publications Company
A division of Lerner Publishing Group
241 First Avenue North
Minneapolis, MN 55401 U.S.A.

Website address: www.lernerbooks.com

Library of Congress Cataloging-in-Publication Data

Savage, Jeff, 1961–
       Albert Pujols / by Jeff Savage.
          p.   cm. — (Amazing athletes)
       Includes index.
       ISBN-13: 978–0–8225–6849–0 (lib. bdg. : alk. paper)
       ISBN-10: 0–8225–6849–7 (lib. bdg. : alk. paper)
       1. Pujols, Albert, 1980– —Juvenile literature. 2. Baseball players—Dominican Republic—
   Biography—Juvenile literature. I. Title.
   GV865.P85S28 2007
   796.357092—dc22 [B]   2006022136

Manufactured in the United States of America
1 2 3 4 5 6 – DP – 12 11 10 09 08 07

TABLE OF CONTENTS

Albert Pujols takes a swing during the St. Louis Cardinals' game against the Houston Astros.

A Winning Blast

Albert Pujols stood in the **batter's box** with a chance to give his team a first-inning lead. Two St. Louis Cardinals were on base with no outs. Albert swung hard at the pitch—and popped it up. The Houston Astros infielder caught the ball for the out.

Albert trudged back to his team's dugout. But instead of sitting down, Albert went to the clubhouse. He watched a tape recording of his swing. He wanted to see what he did wrong. As he watched, he ate a piece of fruit.

It was Game 5 of the 2005 **National League Championship Series (NLCS).** The Cardinals were trailing the series 3 games to 1. The NLCS winner would reach the **World Series.** The Cardinals needed to win this game, or their season would be over.

In the third inning, Albert got another chance. The Cardinals again had two runners on with no outs. This time, Albert struck out. He was angry with himself. He went back to the clubhouse to study more videotape.

Albert walks back to the dugout after striking out in the third inning.

Albert swings at a pitch in the ninth inning.

Albert is his team's best hitter. He is muscular, with quick hands and a smooth swing. He is smart and patient at the plate. He does not swing at every pitch. He knows to wait for a good pitch to hit. But he was struggling now. Twice more, Albert made outs. The game reached the ninth inning. The Cardinals trailed by the score of 4–2.

The first two Cardinals made outs. Then David Eckstein **singled,** and Jim Edmonds **walked.** Albert came to the plate once more. He raised his bat as 43,470 Astros fans screamed for one final out. Brad Lidge threw the pitch. Strike one. Lidge fired the next pitch. Albert uncoiled and swung hard. Boom! The ball sailed high and deep. It landed well beyond the left field seats for a three-run **home run**! The Cardinals stunned the Astros and their fans with a 5–4 victory.

"The game is not over until you get 27 outs," Albert said afterward. "Never give up because anything crazy can happen."

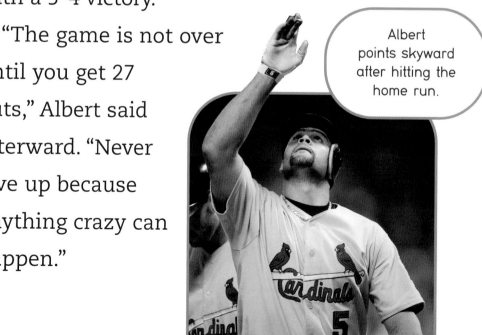

Albert points skyward after hitting the home run.

Baseball is very popular in Santo Domingo, where Albert grew up.

EARNING HIS WAY

Jose Alberto Pujols was born January 16, 1980, in the Dominican Republic, an island country in the Caribbean Sea. Albert grew up poor. He was the youngest of 12 children raised by his mother, America, and his father, Bienvenido. The Pujols family lived in Santo Domingo, the country's capital.

Since Albert was a child, he dreamed of playing big-league baseball. His father pitched in the Dominican **minor leagues.** "I used to wear his uniform whenever I could," said Albert. "I wanted to be like him."

Albert and his friends played baseball on dirt fields. They used limes for baseballs and made gloves out of cardboard milk boxes. Sticks were bats. Albert practiced for hours every day. "I knew if I wanted anything more, I would have to work harder at it," Albert said.

Albert played baseball when he was young, like these boys in the Dominican Republic.

Albert was 16 years old when he moved with his father to the United States. Some of Albert's relatives were already living in Independence, Missouri. Albert and his father lived with Albert's grandmother in Independence. Several aunts and uncles worked nearby as school bus drivers. Albert could hardly believe the riches in the United States. "We come from a poor, poor country," he said. "When we came to the United States, it was like, 'Oh man, we're in heaven!'"

The family enrolled Albert at Fort Osage High School. He could only speak Spanish. "It was tough the first year," Albert said. "I was shy. I knew that I needed English to communicate. So I worked hard at it, just like baseball." Soon, Albert was earning As and Bs in school.

In baseball, Albert earned all-state honors by smashing long home runs. He once hit a ball over the stadium wall and onto the top of a two-story building. He led Fort Osage to the Missouri state championship.

"He was so disciplined," said Albert's teacher, Portia Stanke. "He never ate a cookie or candy. He would say, 'This is not good for me.'"

In 1998, Albert graduated from high school. One night soon after graduation, Albert met a woman named Deidre at a Kansas City dance club. They began dating. Two weeks later, Deidre told Albert about her young daughter, Isabella, who suffered from **Down syndrome.** Deidre explained how the disorder caused learning problems and physical challenges. "He was almost in tears," Deidre said. "His heart was so tender about it."

Albert went to college in Kansas City, Missouri.

MAKING THE JUMP

After high school, Albert played baseball at Maple Woods Community College. Word spread about this new shortstop who banged out long home runs. **Major League Baseball (MLB) scouts** came to see him. In the 13th round of the 1999 **draft,** the Cardinals chose Albert. They offered him $10,000 to sign a **contract.**

Albert knew he was worth more money. He declined the offer. One month later, the Cardinals offered him $60,000. This time, Albert agreed. He joined the Cardinals minor-league system.

On New Year's Day in 2000, Albert and Deidre married. Albert adopted Isabella as his daughter. A son, AJ, and a second daughter, Sophia, have since joined the family.

Albert and his wife, Deidre, attend a news conference.

Albert takes an at-bat during a minor-league game in 2000.

Albert played for the Cardinals' Class A team in Peoria, Illinois. He was paid $126 a week. It was not enough to support his family. To earn more money, Albert worked as a waiter in a restaurant. He also lifted weights two hours every day. "Lifting, lifting, lifting," said Albert. "I worked hard to get stronger."

In March 2001, Albert played with the big-league Cardinals at **spring training.** Major-league teams want to see how players perform against the best pros. It usually takes several years for a player in the minor leagues to move up to the major-league team. Few can make it that far at all.

But Albert impressed everyone with his powerful hitting. One week before the regular season, Albert was in the batter's box again. Cardinals superstar first baseman Mark McGwire was sitting in the dugout with coach Tony La Russa. "What do you think? We going to take him?" McGwire asked the coach. "A lot of us think he should make the club."

Albert and teammate Mark McGwire (right) talk before a game in 2001.

Just then, Albert crushed the next pitch over the wall for another home run.

Albert made the big-league club. He had jumped from Class A straight to the majors. Albert is a religious man, and he never felt more blessed.

As a 21-year-old **rookie,** he played third base, left field, right field, and first base. He blasted balls over the wall. He even made the National League (NL) **All-Star team.** Teammates and fans were amazed. But Albert wasn't amazed. "I don't know if I've surprised other people, but I'm not surprised," he said. "When you work hard, you can't be surprised. When you work hard, you get your goals."

Albert gets one of his many hits of the season during a game against the Detroit Tigers in July 2001.

INSTANT STAR

In his first year on the team, Albert led the Cardinals in hitting. He had a .329 **batting average** with 37 homers, 47 **doubles,** 112 runs scored, and 130 **runs batted in (RBIs).** He was unanimously voted the NL's Rookie of the Year.

Albert worked even harder his second year. He studied videotapes of his at-bats against every pitcher. He practiced his swing in the batting cage three times a day. He learned tips from super hitters such as Alex Rodriguez.

"You learn from your mistakes. Every day you learn something new," Albert said. "That's what you want, to get better and better." When the season ended, Albert had become the first player in baseball history to have in one year better than a .300 average, 30 homers, and 100 runs scored and runs batted in. He finished second in the vote for baseball's Most Valuable Player (MVP), behind San Francisco Giants slugger Barry Bonds.

Albert is a team player. He does not try to win awards for himself. "I don't worry about winning the MVP, the batting title, or home runs. I don't think about that stuff," Albert says. "If you start putting those things in your head, you just put pressure on yourself. You don't want that. You want to keep your mind clear. I just want to get ready to help the team out."

In 2003, Albert finished second to Bonds in the MVP voting again. Albert batted .359 and hit safely in 30 straight games. The streak ended when Albert got sick with the flu. By then, he was one of the most popular players in baseball. He was on the cover of magazines, and he received the most votes for the All-Star Game. Coach La Russa said Albert was the best player he had ever managed. "That's really amazing," Albert said. "But I've got to go out and prove it every day."

Cardinals manager Tony La Russa has been Albert's coach since Albert started in the major leagues.

Albert takes his turn during the Home Run Derby at the 2003 All-Star Game.

The Cardinals were convinced that Albert would work to be one of the greatest players of all time. They signed him to a seven-year contract for $100 million. Albert was rich beyond his wildest dreams. But he did not get carried away with his money. His family lived in a five-bedroom house. He did not need a mansion. "I grew up poor. I never forgot where I came from," he said. "It makes you feel good inside to remember."

The Cardinals celebrate winning the NLCS against the Houston Astros in 2004.

REACHING FOR A RING

Albert seemed to have everything. But there was one thing missing—a World Series ring. In 2004, Albert batted in the middle of a powerful lineup that included Jim Edmonds and Scott Rolen. The Cardinals won a league-best 105 games.

In the **playoffs,** they defeated the Los Angeles Dodgers and the Houston Astros. They reached the World Series. But the Boston Red Sox swept them in four games and won the title. "It was great to be there, but it's too bad the way we played," said Albert, who did all he could. He batted .414 in the playoffs with a team-record six home runs.

After the season, Albert worked out harder than ever. "You don't win a championship with words," he said. "You do it with work."

Albert bats during Game One of the 2004 World Series against the Boston Red Sox.

The Cardinals reached the playoffs again in 2005. This time, they beat the San Diego Padres. They met the Astros again in the NLCS. Albert desperately wanted to get his team another shot

Albert *(right)* celebrates his game-winning home run in Game 5 of the NLCS with teammates David Eckstein *(left)* and Jim Edmonds *(center)*.

at the World Series ring. His home run in Game 5 kept the Cardinals alive.

But the Cardinals lost Game 6 to end their season. Albert did not get his ring, but he did receive another honor—the NL's MVP trophy. He was the first Cardinals player in 20 years to win the award. Albert gave his team the credit. "You have to have a great year by your team to win it," he said. "You can't do it by yourself."

Albert remained focused on the bigger prize. "One massive goal is easier to reach than five smaller ones," he said. "My goal is to win a World Series."

Albert reached his goal in 2006.

Cardinals general manager Walt Jocketty says, "Albert is so focused on what he does. He wants to be the best player in the game, of all time. From the day we signed him to now, he never lets up."

The Cardinals rolled past the San Diego Padres and edged the New York Mets in the playoffs. They made it to the World Series again. This time, they faced the Detroit Tigers. Albert was determined not to let this chance get away. He smacked a two-run home run at Detroit in Game 1 to lead the Cardinals to a 7-2 victory. The Tigers won Game 2 to even the series one win apiece.

Then the Cardinals won three straight games at Busch Stadium in St. Louis to win the title. "Now I can say I have a World

Albert celebrates getting the World Series trophy with his son, AJ, on his shoulders.

Before a game in 2006, Albert sits with his family, wife Deidre *(left)*, and children *(left to right)* Sophia, Isabella, and AJ.

Series ring in my trophy case," Albert said. "And that's what you play for."

Albert continues to shine in baseball. He also devotes time to his family. Together they go out for pizza or to the movies. He reads to Isabella, AJ, and Sophia every night. "Daddy, you wear number 5, right?" AJ often asks. "Yes," Albert says. "And you play baseball, right, Daddy?" "Yes," Albert replies.

AJ already knows the answers, of course. He just likes to ask and have his father tell him again. Albert takes time to work with Isabella too. He and Deidre actively raise funds for Down syndrome research.

Albert is quiet and shy. Still, he takes time to speak to minor leaguers. "It's in my heart," he says. "I want to help those kids out. I love the game."

Albert enjoys giving young Latin American players advice. "I know how tough it is to come here knowing no English," Albert says. "You don't need to give money to these kids. You just need to encourage them to keep working hard and take advantage of the opportunities they get."

Selected Career Highlights

2006 Won his first Gold Glove
Named starter at first base for the NL in the All-Star Game
Hit a career-high 49 home runs
Ranked second in MLB in RBIs (137)
Ranked third in the NL in batting average (.331)

2005 Named NL MVP
Named starter at first base for the NL in the All-Star Game
Led the NL in runs scored (129)
Ranked second in the NL in batting average (.330) and runs batted
  in (117)
Ranked third in the NL in home runs (41)

2004 Finished third in NL MVP voting
Named starter at first base for the NL in the All-Star Game
Led the NL in runs scored (133)
Ranked third in the NL in runs batted in (123)
Ranked fifth in the NL in batting average (.331)
Hit 46 home runs

2003 Finished second in NL MVP voting

2002 Finished second in NL MVP voting

2001 As a rookie, led the Cardinals with a
    .329 average, 37 home runs,
    and 130 runs batted in
Named NL Rookie of the Year
Finished fourth in NL MVP voting

2000 Batted .314 for three St. Louis
    Cardinals minor league teams

1999 Named Junior College All-America as
    a shortstop

1998 Led Fort Osage High School to
    Missouri state championship
Received all-state honors in baseball

1997 Received all-state honors in baseball

Glossary

All-Star team: a group of the best players, as voted by the fans. They compete in a special game each year.

batter's box: the area next to home plate in which the batter stands

batting average: a number that describes how often a baseball player makes a base hit

contract: a written deal between a player and a team or a company

doubles: hits that allow batters to safely reach second base

Down syndrome: a condition at birth that causes slowed growth, different facial features, and some mental retardation

draft: a yearly event in which professional teams take turns choosing new players from a selected group

home run: a hit that allows the batter to circle all the bases and score a run

Major League Baseball (MLB): the top group of professional men's baseball teams in North America, divided into the National League and the American League

minor leagues: groups of teams in which players improve their skills and prepare to move to the majors

MLB scouts: people who judge the skills of players. Scouts work for individual teams and help them decide who to draft.

National League Championship Series (NLCS): a set of games played at the end of the baseball season between the two top National League teams. The team that wins four games goes to the World Series to play the winner of the American League Championship Series (ALCS).

playoffs: games played to decide which team is the Major League Baseball champion

rookie: a player who is playing his or her first season

runs batted in (RBIs): the number of runners able to score on a batter's hit or walk

singled: a play in which the batter safely reached first base on a hit

spring training: a time from February through March when baseball teams train for the season

walked: a play in which the batter reached first base by taking four pitches outside the strike zone

World Series: MLB's championship. The winning teams from the National League and the American League play each other in the World Series.

Further Reading & Websites

Horn, Geoffrey. *Albert Pujols*. Milwaukee: Gareth Stevens, 2006.

Major League Baseball
http://www.mlb.com
Major League Baseball's official website provides fans with the latest scores and game schedules, as well as information on players, teams, and baseball history.

Pujols Family Foundation
http://www.pujolsfamilyfoundation.org
The official homepage of the Pujols Family Foundation describes Albert and Deidre's charitable work. The foundation raises money for children with Down syndrome, disabilities, and serious illnesses. It also raises money for children living in poor conditions in the Dominican Republic.

Sports Illustrated for Kids
http://www.sikids.com
The *Sports Illustrated for Kids* website covers all sports, including baseball.

St. Louis Cardinals: The Official Site
http://stlouis.cardinals.mlb.com
The official website of the St. Louis Cardinals includes the team schedule and game results, late-breaking news, biographies of Albert Pujols and other players and coaches, and much more.

Index

Photo Acknowledgments

The images in this book are used with the permission of: © Ronald Martinez/Getty Images, pp. 4, 6; AP Images/David J. Phillip, p. 7; © Elsa/Getty Images, p. 8; © Peter Power/Toronto Star/ZUMA Press, p. 9; © Tom Bean/CORBIS, p. 10; © Richard Cummins/CORBIS, p. 13; AP Images/James A. Finley, p. 14; © Diamond Images/Getty Images, p. 15; © Scott Rovak/AFP/Getty Images, p. 16; © Steve Boyle/NewSport/CORBIS, p. 18; © Stephen Dunn/Getty Images, p. 20; © Jonathan Daniel/Getty Images, pp. 21, 22; © Ron Vesely/MLB Photos via Getty Images, p. 23; © Thomas B. Shea/USP/ZUMA Press, p. 24; © Jed Jacobsohn/Getty Images, p. 26; © John Grieshop/MLB Photos via Getty Images, p. 27; © Jim McIsaac/Getty Images, p. 29.

Front cover: © Ed Wolfstein/Icon SMI